D0938628

I Love Sports

Golf

by Cari Meister

Bullfrog Books

Ideas for Parents and Teachers

Bullfrog Books let children practice reading informational text at the earliest reading levels. Repetition, familiar words, and photo labels support early readers.

Before Reading

- Discuss the cover photo. What does it tell them?

- Look at the picture glossary together. Read and discuss the words.

Read the Book

- "Walk" through the book and look at the photos. Let the child ask questions. Point out the photo labels.

- Read the book to the child, or have him or her read independently.

After Reading

- Prompt the child to think more. Ask: Have you ever gone golfing? Did you enjoy it?

Bullfrog Books are published by Jump!
5357 Penn Avenue South
Minneapolis, MN 55419
www.jumplibrary.com

Library of Congress Cataloging-in-Publication Data

Names: Meister, Cari.
Title: Golf / by Cari Meister.
Description: Minneapolis, MN: Jump!, Inc. [2017]
Series: Bullfrog Books. I Love Sports
Includes index. | Audience: Ages: 5–8.
Audience: Grades: K to Grade 3.
Identifiers: LCCN 2016008936 (print)
LCCN 2016009461 (ebook)
ISBN 9781620313596 (hardcover: alk. paper)
ISBN 9781624964060 (ebook)
Subjects: LCSH: Golf—Juvenile literature.
Classification: LCC GV968 .M45 2016 (print)
LCC GV968 (ebook) | DDC 796.352—dc23
LC record available at http://lccn.loc.gov/2016008936

Editor: Jenny Fretland VanVoorst
Series Designer: Ellen Huber
Book Designer: Molly Ballanger
Photo Researcher: Molly Ballanger

Photo Credits: All photos by Shutterstock except:
Getty, 8; iStock, 6–7, 14–15, 23bl; SuperStock, 20–21;
Thinkstock, 22.

Printed in the United States of America at Corporate Graphics in North Mankato, Minnesota.

The creative director dedicates this book to the Evans Scholar Foundation.

Table of Contents

Let's Golf!

Get your clubs.

Put on sunblock.

Let's golf!

5

Ani looks at
the fairway.

It is a long
way to the pin.

Which club
should she use?

pin

driver

Ani gets a driver.
She swings.

The ball soars.

Oh, no!
The ball lands
in a bunker.

bunker

TJ is up.

He puts a ball on a tee.

He swings.

tee ·····▶

13

Ani and TJ
walk to the balls.

Ani chips her ball.

It goes out
of the sand.

15

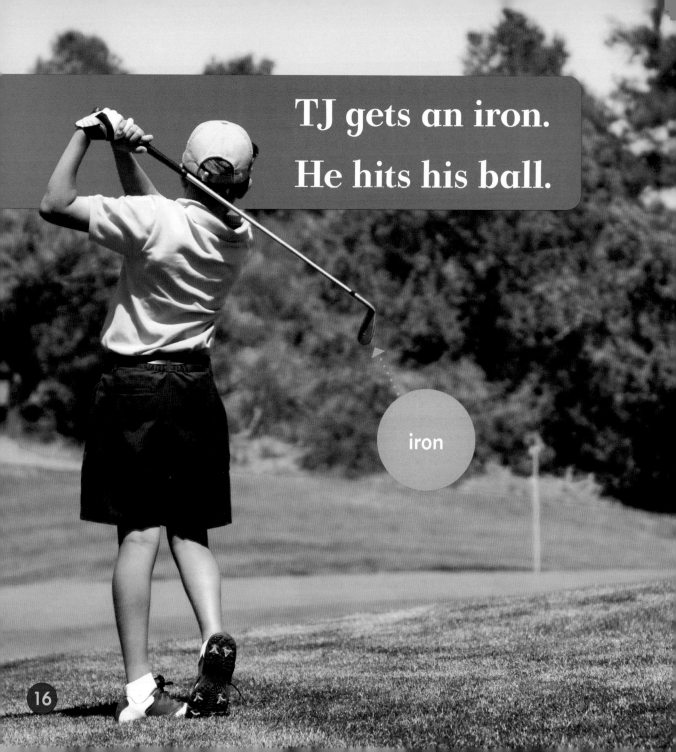

TJ gets an iron.
He hits his ball.

iron

16

It lands on the green!

Now they are
on the green.

They get putters.

They take turns.

They tap the balls
into the hole.

putter

hole

Do you want to play?

Grab your clubs.

Grab a ball.

Golf is fun!

On the Golf Course

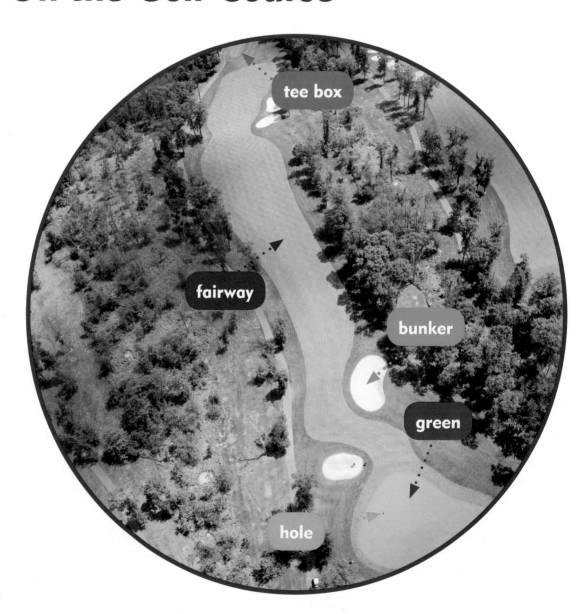

tee box

fairway

bunker

green

hole

Picture Glossary

bunker
A hollow hazard on a golf course that contains sand.

iron
Golf clubs with smaller heads than drivers, used for hitting the ball different distances.

chip
To hit the ball in a way that lofts the ball to the green and allows it to roll.

putter
The golf club used to hit the ball very short distances on the green.

driver
A golf club with a big head, used for hitting the ball a long distance.

tee
A small piece of wood stuck in the ground used to hold up a golf ball.

Index

To Learn More

Learning more is as easy as 1, 2, 3.

1) Go to www.factsurfer.com

2) Enter "golf" into the search box.

3) Click the "Surf" button to see a list of websites.

With factsurfer.com, finding more information is just a click away.